The Quantum Leap

Leap

Google's Revolutionary Willow Chip

A Detailed Look at the Groundbreaking
Technology and Its Impact on the Future of
Computing

Joe E. Grayson

Disclaimer:

The information contained in this book is provided for general informational purposes only. While every effort has been made to ensure that the information is accurate and up-to-date, The Author makes no representations or warranties of any kind, express or implied, about the completeness, accuracy, reliability, suitability, or availability with respect to the information, products, services, or related graphics contained in the book for any purpose.

The Author disclaims any liability for any loss or damage, including without limitation, indirect or consequential loss or damage, or any loss or damage whatsoever arising from loss of data or profits arising out of, or in connection with, the use of this book.

Readers are solely responsible for determining the appropriateness of the information contained in this book for their specific purposes and should seek professional advice before acting upon any information contained herein. The Author shall not be liable for any damages of any kind arising from the use of this book or the information contained herein.

Table of Contents

Introduction

In today's digital age, cybersecurity has become more important than ever before. As we rely on technology more and more to do our daily tasks, cyber threats become increasingly prevalent. It's crucial that we understand the terminology associated with cybersecurity in order to effectively protect our personal information and assets. This glossary-type book provides a comprehensive overview of the most important concepts and terms in cybersecurity. Whether you're an IT professional, business owner or simply someone who wants to stay informed about digital security, this book is a must-read.

Access Control

The process of limiting and controlling the access to data, systems, or applications to prevent unauthorized use or modification. This includes authorization, authentication, and accountability measures.

Adversary

A malicious agent or entity that performs attacks, exploits vulnerabilities, or steals data from a system or network. This can be a hacker, a malware, a cybercriminal, or an insider threat.

Anomaly Detection

The process of identifying unusual or abnormal behaviors, patterns, or events in a system or network that might indicate a security breach or attack. This is done through statistical analysis, machine learning, or other techniques.

Antivirus Software

A type of software that protects computer systems from malware, viruses, spyware, adware, and other malicious software that can harm or steal sensitive data.

Application Security

The process of designing, testing, and implementing secure software applications that are free from vulnerabilities, bugs, or weaknesses that could be exploited by attackers. This includes secure coding practices, threat modeling, and vulnerability assessment.

Asset

Any resource or data that has value, whether tangible or intangible, such as hardware, software, information, or intellectual property. Protecting assets is a critical part of cybersecurity.

Attack Surface

The sum of all attack vectors or vulnerabilities that can be exploited by attackers to gain access or control of a system or application.

Audit Trail

A record of events, transactions, or activities in a system or network that provides evidence of compliance, accountability, or anomalies. This is useful for forensic investigations, compliance, and risk management.

Authentication

The process of verifying the identity of a user or system to grant access to resources or data. This can be achieved through passwords, biometrics, or multi-factor authentication methods.

Awareness Training

The process of educating users, employees, or stakeholders about cybersecurity risks, best practices, policies, and procedures. This helps to create a culture of security, reduce human errors or mistakes, and improve overall cybersecurity posture.

Backup

A backup is a copy of data that can be used to recover information in case the original data is lost or damaged. Backups are an essential part of cybersecurity because they allow organizations to restore data and systems quickly after a cyberattack or other disaster. Backups should be created regularly, stored securely, and tested periodically to ensure they are effective.

Beaconing

Beaconing refers to the process by which malware sends a periodic signal to a command and control (C&C) server to indicate that it is still active and waiting for instructions. Beaconing is a common tactic used by advanced persistent threats (APTs) and other sophisticated malware to evade detection and maintain persistence. Organizations can detect and respond to beaconing by monitoring network traffic for unusual outgoing connections or traffic patterns.

Bot

A bot is an automated program or script that performs tasks on behalf of a user or system. Bots can be used for many legitimate purposes, such as web crawling and chatbots, but they can also be used for malicious purposes, such as spreading malware or performing DDoS attacks. Organizations can defend against malicious bots by implementing measures such as CAPTCHA tests, bot detection software, and web application firewalls.

Botnet

A botnet is a network of compromised computers that can be controlled by an attacker. Botnets are often used for malicious activities such as spamming, distributed denial of service (DDoS) attacks, and credential theft. Organizations can defend against botnets by maintaining strong security controls, such as up-to-date antivirus software and firewalls, and by monitoring network traffic for signs of botnet activity.

Brute force attack

A brute force attack is a method of cracking a password or encryption key by trying every possible combination until the correct one is found. Brute force attacks can be time-consuming and resource-intensive, but they are still a common method used by hackers to gain unauthorized access to systems or data. Organizations can protect against brute force attacks by implementing strong passwords policies, limiting the number of login attempts, and using multi-factor authentication.

Bug bounty

A bug bounty is a program offered by a software or website developer that rewards individuals for finding and reporting vulnerabilities. Bug bounty programs are becoming increasingly popular as a way for organizations to identify and address security vulnerabilities before they can be exploited by hackers. Participants in bug bounty programs may receive monetary rewards, recognition, or other incentives for their contributions.

BYOD

BYOD stands for Bring Your Own Device. It refers to the practice of employees using their personal devices, such as smartphones, tablets, and laptops, for work purposes. BYOD can pose a security risk because personal devices may not have the same security controls as corporate devices, and because they may be used on unsecured networks. Organizations can mitigate these risks by implementing BYOD policies that set clear guidelines for device use and security, and by using mobile device management (MDM) software to monitor and control access.

Cloud security

The practice of protecting cloud-based applications, data, and infrastructure from cyber threats through various security mechanisms such as encryption, access controls, and continuous monitoring. It ensures the secure and reliable operation of cloud services.

Compliance

The adherence to laws, regulations, and industry standards that govern cybersecurity practices, including data privacy laws such as GDPR and HIPAA, and cybersecurity frameworks such as NIST and ISO.

Confidentiality

The principle of ensuring that sensitive information is kept secret and only accessible to authorized individuals or entities, thus preventing unauthorized disclosure or exposure of sensitive data that could harm individuals or organizations.

Countermeasures

The actions taken to counter or mitigate potential cyber threats, including incident response, individual and network-level security measures, and security awareness training.

Cryptography

The practice of secure communication that involves converting data into a code to prevent unauthorized access, manipulation, or theft. It uses various algorithms such as AES, RSA, and SHA to secure data.

Cyber hygiene

The practice of maintaining good cybersecurity habits and best practices such as updating software, using strong passwords, and educating employees to prevent cyber threats.

Cyber insurance

The insurance policy that provides financial protection to individuals or organizations against losses or damages caused by cyber attacks, data breaches, or other cyber-related incidents.

Cyber threat intelligence (CTI)

The information gathered about potential cyber threats and attackers, including their motivations, tactics, and potential impact on targeted individuals or organizations. It helps organizations to proactively identify and prevent cyber attacks.

Cyberattack

A malicious attempt to disrupt, damage, or gain unauthorized access to a computer system, network, or device via various techniques such as malware, phishing, and denial-of-service (DoS) attacks.

Cybersecurity

The practice of protecting computer systems, networks, and sensitive information from unauthorized access, theft, and damage by identifying and addressing potential security risks through various security measures such as firewalls, encryption, and multi-factor authentication.

Dark Web

A hidden part of the internet that is inaccessible using traditional search engines. The dark web is often used for illegal activities, including the sale of stolen data, drugs and weapons.

Data Encryption

The process of converting plaintext data into an unreadable form to protect it from unauthorized access during transmission or storage. Encryption ensures that unauthorized parties cannot access or understand the data even if they gain access to it.

Denial of Service (DoS) Attack

A type of cyber attack aimed at making a website, network or computer system unavailable to users by flooding it with traffic until it crashes or runs out of resources. This can result in loss of revenue and reputation damage.

Digital Forensics

The use of specialized tools and techniques to investigate and gather evidence from digital devices such as computers, mobile phones, and storage devices. Digital forensics is used in cybercrime investigations to identify and prosecute criminals.

DNS Spoofing

A type of cyber attack where a hacker hijacks the Domain Name System (DNS) and redirects users to fake websites. This can lead to the stealing of sensitive information, such as credit card numbers and social security numbers.

Electronic Warfare

A branch of military action that involves the use of electronics and information technology to disrupt or attack electronic systems. Electronic warfare includes activities such as jamming, interception, and intrusion of communication systems. It is used by various governments and military organizations to ensure national security and to protect critical infrastructure such as power grids, transportation systems, and financial networks.

Email Security

A set of techniques and tools used to protect email communication from cyber threats. Email security solutions include spam filters, anti-malware, antivirus, and encryption. It also includes the use of digital signatures and certificates to authenticate the sender's identity and ensure the integrity of the message. Email security solutions also prevent sensitive information from being transmitted in plain text and limit the risk of social engineering attacks such as phishing.

Encryption

A process of encoding information to protect it from unauthorized access. Encryption uses complex algorithms to convert plain text into a coded message, which is only readable by authorized individuals who possess the decryption key. It is an essential component of cybersecurity as it ensures the confidentiality of sensitive information such as passwords, credit card details, and other confidential data. Encryption techniques such as AES, RSA, and Blowfish are widely used in various applications such as email communications, mobile devices, and online transactions.

Encryption Algorithm

A set of rules and procedures used to encrypt and decrypt data. Encryption algorithms are critical in cybersecurity as they ensure the confidentiality of sensitive information. Encryption algorithms use complex mathematical algorithms to transform plain text into cipher text, which is only readable with the decryption key. Examples of encryption algorithms include AES, RSA, and Blowfish. Encryption algorithms are continually evolving, and it is essential to use the latest standards to stay ahead of cyber threats.

Encryption Key

A unique code that is used to encrypt and decrypt data in cryptography. Encryption keys are essential to secure data by ensuring that sensitive information can only be accessed by authorized individuals. Encryption keys are generated using advanced algorithms, and their strength determines the level of security provided. Encryption keys can be stored securely using a hardware security module or a key management system to ensure their protection.

Endpoint Detection and Response (EDR)

A cybersecurity solution that provides real-time monitoring and response to endpoint security incidents. EDR solutions include endpoint security agents, advanced analytics, and machine learning to detect and respond to security threats. EDR solutions provide visibility into endpoint activity to detect suspicious behavior and to investigate security incidents. EDR solutions also provide incident response playbooks to guide security teams in response to incidents, and to prevent future incidents.

Endpoint Security

A practice of securing endpoints, such as laptops, smartphones, and servers from cyber threats. Endpoint security solutions protect against various attacks such as malware, ransomware, and phishing. It provides a layered approach to security that includes antivirus and anti-malware, intrusion detection, data encryption, and firewall protection. Endpoint security solutions also allow organizations to enforce security policies and monitor endpoints for suspicious activities, ensuring that all endpoints are compliant with security protocols.

Ethical Hacking

A process of testing computer systems or networks to identify vulnerabilities and weaknesses in security. Ethical hackers use the same techniques as cybercriminals to detect and exploit vulnerabilities. However, their objective is to improve security by identifying and reporting vulnerabilities to the organization. Ethical hackers simulate attacks to identify weaknesses in systems and networks, and to validate the effectiveness of security measures in place.

Exploit

A piece of software code or a technique that takes advantage of a vulnerability or weakness in a system or application. Attackers use exploits to gain unauthorized access to computers or networks to steal sensitive data, install malware, or disrupt services. Exploits can be delivered through various sources such as malicious email attachments, infected websites, and unpatched software vulnerabilities. It is essential to keep all software and systems up-to-date with security patches to prevent unauthorized access.

External Threats

Cyber threats that originate from outside an organization. External threats can include various attack types such as malware, phishing, ransomware, and advanced persistent threats (APTs). These attacks are usually carried out by cybercriminals, hacktivists, or state-sponsored actors. External threats pose a significant risk to organizations, and it is essential to implement comprehensive security measures to protect against them.

Faraday Cage

A metallic enclosure designed to block electromagnetic waves. Faraday cages can be used to protect electronic devices from electromagnetic interference, but they can also be used to prevent signal transmission to and from a device, making it useful for securing sensitive information.

File Encryption

A process of converting readable data into unreadable code in order to protect its confidentiality. Encryption algorithms break down the data into pieces and then use a key to scramble it. Decryption requires the same key to unscramble the data.

Firewall

A security system designed to monitor and filter incoming and outgoing network traffic. It acts as a barrier between two networks and determines which network traffic is allowed or blocked based on a set of predefined rules.

Firewall Rule

A set of criteria that determine how a firewall should handle incoming or outgoing traffic. Firewall rules can be customized to allow or block specific types of traffic based on port, protocol, IP address, etc.

Firmware

A type of software that is permanently stored in hardware such as a computer motherboard or a router. Firmware provides the necessary instructions for the hardware to operate and is not easily modifiable by the user.

Flaw

A weakness or vulnerability within a system that can be exploited by cybercriminals. Flaws can occur in hardware, software, or in a combination of both, and can result in unintended behavior or security breaches.

Forensics

A branch of science that deals with the collection, preservation, analysis, and presentation of evidence from digital devices. Cyber forensics is used to investigate cybercrimes and help law enforcement agencies prosecute cybercriminals.

Four-factor Authentication

A method of authentication that requires the user to provide four different types of credentials

Fraud

A criminal activity in which someone intentionally deceives another person or business for personal gain. Cyber fraud can include phishing schemes, identity theft, and other types of financial scams.

FTP

File Transfer Protocol. It is a standard network protocol for transferring files from one computer to another over the internet. It allows you to upload and download files between computers and can be secured with encryption.

Gateway

A gateway is a network node that acts as an entrance to another network. It typically connects a LAN (Local Area Network) to a WAN (Wide Area Network) or the internet. Gateways are used to manage traffic between networks, route data packets, and provide security and firewall services.

Hacker

A person who gains unauthorized access to a computer system for malicious purposes. Hackers often use techniques such as phishing, social engineering, and brute force attacks to gain access to sensitive information. Hackers can also install malware and ransomware on systems to hold files hostage or steal personal and financial data. It is essential to take measures to protect against hackers, such as using strong passwords, regularly updating software, and deploying firewalls and antivirus programs.

Hardware Firewall

A network security device that operates within the physical layer of a network. Hardware firewalls examine incoming and outgoing network traffic and block unauthorized access to a system. Hardware firewalls are more secure than software firewalls as they run independently and are not susceptible to malware attacks.

Hash Function

A mathematical algorithm that converts plaintext data to a fixed-size string of characters, called the hash value. Hash functions are commonly used to verify the authenticity and integrity of data, such as passwords, as even a small change in the input data will result in a vastly different output hash value.

Heuristic Analysis

A cybersecurity technique used to identify and analyze previously unknown malware threats. Heuristic analysis involves dynamically analyzing code behavior, utilizing machine learning algorithms to identify patterns and signatures. Heuristic analysis is regularly used in antivirus and intrusion detection software to detect and prevent newly emerging threats.

Honey Pot

A decoy cybersecurity mechanism designed to detect and deter unauthorized access to a system. Honey pots simulate vulnerable systems to lure attackers into engaging with them. Honey pots allow security teams to observe how hackers operate and gather intelligence on their techniques, tactics, and procedures. However, honey pots can also be a double-edged sword as they can attract attackers to valuable systems.

Honeypot Network

A network composed of interconnected honey pots. Honeypot networks are used to identify, track, and analyze malicious activity and observe hacker behavior. Honeypot networks can provide valuable intelligence to security teams but can also be targets of attacks.

Host

A computer or device connected to a network. Hosts are identified by their unique IP addresses, which can be either dynamic or static. Hosts can be vulnerable to cyber threats such as malware, viruses, and phishing attacks. Ensuring host security is essential in maintaining a secure network.

Https

Hypertext Transfer Protocol Secure, a protocol used to secure communications on the internet. HTTPS uses TLS or SSL cryptographic protocols to encrypt data transmitted between a web server and a client device, such as a web browser. HTTPS provides end-to-end encryption, preventing eavesdropping, and tampering of data in transit.

Human Error

A frequent cause of security breaches, resulting from accidental or unintentional actions taken by employees, contractors or associates. Human error can be the result of an absence of cybersecurity training, lack of adherence to security policies, or a lack of awareness of the importance of security. Education and training of all stakeholders within an organization about cybersecurity best practices are critical in reducing the risk of human error cybersecurity breaches.

Hybrid Cloud

A cloud computing environment that operates by combining public and private cloud infrastructures. Hybrid cloud solutions provide the flexibility and scalability of public clouds and the security and control of private clouds. However, hybrid clouds also come with additional security challenges as they rely on multiple interconnected environments.

Identity management

The process of identifying and verifying users' identities to ensure that only authorized individuals have access to digital resources. It includes authentication, authorization, and access control mechanisms that enable users to securely access information, applications, and services. Identity management solutions are used to centralize and automate user access management to increase security and streamline operations.

Incident response

A process that outlines the steps to be taken when a cybersecurity breach occurs. It includes identifying the source and nature of the attack, isolating affected systems, and implementing measures to prevent future incidents. Incident response plans are important for minimizing the impact of breaches, as they enable organizations to quickly and effectively contain incidents and restore normal operations.

Information governance

The framework and processes that manage and protect sensitive data within an organization. It includes policies, standards, and procedures that ensure the confidentiality, integrity, and availability of information, as well as compliance with regulatory requirements. A robust information governance program helps organizations minimize risk, improve decision-making, and establish trust with clients and partners.

Information security

A set of practices and measures designed to protect the
confidentiality, integrity, and availability of digital
information. This includes protecting against unauthorized
access, mitigating risks, and ensuring the privacy of sensitive
data. Information security is a critical aspect of cybersecurity
and is essential for maintaining trust and confidence in
digital systems, especially in sensitive industries such as
financial services and healthcare.

Insider threat

A cybersecurity risk that arises from employees, contractors,
or other trusted individuals within an organization who
intentionally or unintentionally cause harm to the
company's systems, data, or reputation. Insider threats can
result from negligence, human error, or malicious intent
and can be difficult to detect and prevent. Having strong
policies, training programs, and monitoring systems in place
can reduce the risk of insider threats.

Intellectual property

The legal rights and protections afforded to creators of original works, such as patents, trademarks, and copyrights. Intellectual property is often a target of cyberattacks, as cybercriminals seek to steal or misuse proprietary information for financial gain or competitive advantage. Protecting intellectual property requires comprehensive security measures and requires legal action against those who violate intellectual property rights.

Internet of Things (IoT)

A network of interconnected devices that communicate with each other and the internet, collecting and sharing data to automate processes and create new insights. IoT devices are often vulnerable to cybersecurity threats, as they are designed for low-power consumption and may lack adequate security measures. Securing IoT systems is essential for protecting against new forms of cyberattacks and improving the overall security posture of organizations.

Intrusion detection system

A security tool that monitors network activity for signs of suspicious behavior or unauthorized access. It can identify intrusions by analyzing network traffic, logs, and system events. The system provides alerts to security teams when it detects potential intrusion attempts, allowing them to take action before the attack can cause harm.

Jailbreaking

Jailbreaking refers to the process of bypassing the restrictions imposed by the manufacturer or the operator on electronic devices like smartphones, tablets or gaming consoles. This is often done in order to gain access to software or features that are not normally available. However, jailbreaking can leave the device vulnerable to security attacks as the security measures put in place by the manufacturer are bypassed. Jailbreaking can also void warranties and can create instability in the device's operating system.

Java

Java is a programming language commonly used in web development. It is known for its versatility and portability, as it can be run on multiple platforms. However, Java also has a history of security vulnerabilities which can be exploited by attackers. It is important to keep Java up to date to avoid security breaches.

Java Virtual Machine (JVM)

The Java Virtual Machine is a critical component of the Java programming language that allows Java code to be run on multiple platforms. The JVM provides a secure environment for executing Java code, but it can also be a target for attackers who wish to exploit vulnerabilities in the Java runtime environment.

JavaScript

JavaScript is a scripting language used in web development to create interactive user interfaces and dynamic web content. While JavaScript itself is not inherently insecure, it can be used to exploit vulnerabilities in other parts of a website, such as poorly secured forms or login pages. It is important to ensure that any code containing JavaScript is thoroughly vetted and tested to ensure that it is secure.

Jitter

Jitter refers to the variation in delay between the transmission and reception of a data packet over a network. High levels of jitter can result in poor network performance and can make it more difficult to ensure the security and reliability of data transmitted over the network.

Job-Based Access Control (JBAC)

Job-based access control is a method of controlling user access to resources based on their job role within an organization. Users are given access to only the resources that are necessary for them to perform their job functions, reducing the risk of unauthorized access and potential security breaches.

John the Ripper

John the Ripper is a password cracking tool used by cybersecurity professionals to test the strength of passwords. It is a command-line tool that is used to crack passwords by identifying common patterns used by users, such as common phrases or simple number combinations. John the Ripper can be used to identify weak passwords in an organization's network and can help enforce stronger password policies.

Joint Interoperability Test Command (JITC)

The Joint Interoperability Test Command is a United States Department of Defense organization responsible for testing and evaluating IT systems for use in the military. This includes evaluating the security of the systems to ensure that they meet the strict security requirements imposed by the U.S. government.

JSON Web Token (JWT)

JSON Web Tokens are a type of token used for authentication and authorization in web applications. They allow user information to be securely transmitted between the client and server in a compact and self-contained format. However, JWTs can also be vulnerable to security attacks if proper measures are not taken to ensure that they are securely transmitted and validated.

Just in Time (JIT) Compilation

Just in Time compilation refers to a process used in programming where code is compiled and executed at runtime rather than being compiled ahead of time. This can result in increased application speed and improved memory management, but it can also create security vulnerabilities if the code is not thoroughly vetted for security flaws.

Kerberos

A network authentication protocol that uses a ticket-granting system to verify the identity of users and services. This protocol restricts access to resources to authorized users and protects against unauthorized access by using a shared secret key. Kerberos is widely used in enterprise environments and is considered a reliable authentication mechanism, however, it is vulnerable to certain types of attacks such as brute-force attacks and credential theft.

Kernel

The central component of an operating system that manages system resources such as memory, hardware, and software. The kernel provides a layer of security by isolating different processes from one another and protecting against unauthorized access. Kernel-level attacks are a significant threat to cybersecurity as they can bypass many of the operating system's security mechanisms.

Key Escrow

A process of storing cryptographic keys with a third-party service provider for backup and recovery purposes. Key escrow is often required by government agencies or in regulated industries where access to data needs to be maintained even if the original keys are lost or damaged. However, key escrow can also be a vulnerability if the third-party service provider is compromised, as it exposes sensitive data to potential attackers.

Key Exchange

The process by which two or more parties exchange cryptographic keys to establish a secure communication channel. The keys are used to encrypt and decrypt messages, and to authenticate the identity of the parties involved. Key exchange protocols, such as Diffie-Hellman, are critical for ensuring the confidentiality and integrity of data in transit.

Key Length

The number of bits used to create a cryptographic key. Longer keys provide better security as they increase the number of possible combinations of the key, making it harder to crack. The appropriate key length depends on the cryptographic algorithm used and the level of security required. For example, the recommended key length for RSA encryption is at least 2048 bits.

Key Management

A process of generating, storing, distributing, and revoking cryptographic keys used for encryption, decryption, and digital signing. Effective key management is critical for maintaining the overall security of a system as compromised keys can lead to the loss of confidentiality and integrity of sensitive data. It is especially important in large-scale systems and enterprises where a large number of keys need to be managed across multiple devices and networks.

Key Stretching

A technique used to improve the security of cryptographic keys by making them harder to attack. It involves running the key through a series of mathematical functions that increase the amount of time and computing power required to attack the key. Key stretching is essential for protecting sensitive data from brute-force attacks and should be used whenever possible.

Key Verification

A process of verifying the authenticity of cryptographic keys before they are used. Key verification ensures that the keys have not been tampered with or changed in transit, and that they belong to the intended recipient. This process is critical for ensuring the integrity and confidentiality of encrypted data and for preventing man-in-the-middle attacks. Key verification can be accomplished using digital certificates or other secure communication channels.

Keylogger

A program or device that records keystrokes on a computer keyboard without the user's knowledge. It is often used by hackers to steal sensitive information such as passwords, usernames, and credit card details. Keyloggers are a major issue for cybersecurity as they can be difficult to detect and can capture a large amount of data over time, posing significant threats to personal and business security.

Known Vulnerability

A security flaw or weakness that has been identified and published, and for which a patch or fix is available. Known vulnerabilities pose a significant risk to cybersecurity as they can be exploited by attackers who have access to the exploit code. Organizations should regularly update their systems with security patches to minimize the risk of known vulnerabilities being exploited.

Lateral Movement

The movement of cyber attackers within a network after the initial breach. After gaining access to a system or device, attackers will attempt to spread their reach further into the network, using various tactics to exploit vulnerabilities and move laterally. This movement enables attackers to maintain persistence, compromise additional assets and gain access to sensitive information. Cybersecurity experts utilize various strategies, such as network segmentation and endpoint protection, to reduce the risks of lateral movement.

Layered Security

The use of multiple security measures and approaches to protect against cyber threats. The goal of layered security is to make it difficult for attackers to penetrate the network, by implementing various security controls at multiple levels. The layers might include firewalls, intrusion detection systems, anti-malware software, and other network and endpoint protections.

Least Privilege Principle

A fundamental principle of cybersecurity that restricts the level of access and privileges that users, applications, or systems have within a network. The principle seeks to limit potential damage by ensuring that all users and applications only have the minimal access required to complete their specific tasks. Access control mechanisms, such as authentication and authorization protocols, enforce this principle to limit the exposure of sensitive information and prevent unauthorized access.

Log Monitoring

The process of overseeing and analyzing system logs for potential security issues or irregular activity. Logs are crucial sources of data that provide insight into network and device activities, offering a way to detect issues before they cause damage. Security teams use log monitoring tools to track security events, such as failed login attempts or malware infections, and alert analysts to take action when necessary.

Malware

A type of software designed to harm a computer system, network, or mobile device. Malware can infiltrate a device through malicious emails, pop-up ads, and attachments. It can cause data loss or theft, slow down a device's performance, and even take control of it. There are several types of malware, including viruses, Trojan horses, worms, and ransomware, all of which require different types of protection to defend against.

Man-in-the-middle attack

A cyber-attack where an attacker intercepts communications between two parties to steal data or alter it. This type of attack takes place when a user sends data to another user or a server, and a third-party intercepts and modifies the data in transit, without being detected. Such an attack can be prevented by using encryption, authentication, strong firewall, anti-malware protection, and regular software updates.

Mitigation

The process of reducing the severity or impact of a cyber-attack. It involves taking steps to prevent an attack from occurring or to minimize its impact if it occurs. Some mitigation strategies include regular backups, website security scans, hardening network infrastructure, and training users about cyber threats and how to avoid them.

Multi-factor authentication

An additional layer of security to protect a user's digital identity. It is the practice of requiring two or more different types of authentication factors, such as a password and a fingerprint or a security token, to verify a user's identity. Multi-factor authentication makes it harder for attackers to gain access to an account, as they have to bypass two or more authentication steps.

NAC

Network Access Control (NAC) is a security technology that manages network access by enforcing policies and rules for endpoint devices that connect to the network. NAC solutions can ensure that only authenticated and authorized devices can access the network, and they can enforce security policies such as restricting access to certain resources or ensuring that antivirus software is installed and up to date.

Nacld

Network Access Control List (NACLD) is a security feature that defines rules and policies for controlling access to network resources. NACLDs are typically implemented in routers and switches and can be used to restrict traffic based on criteria such as source and destination IP addresses, port numbers, or protocols. NACLDs can be used to prevent unauthorized access and to protect network resources against malicious activity.

NACM

Network Access Control Model (NACM) is a security model that defines rules and policies for controlling access to network resources. NACM is based on the principle of least privilege, which means that users are granted only the access they need to perform their jobs. NACM can prevent unauthorized access and reduce the risk of data breaches by ensuring that only authorized users have access to sensitive information.

Namespace

A namespace is a concept in computer science that refers to a way of organizing and grouping objects together. In the context of cybersecurity, namespaces are used to provide a logical structure and naming convention for security policies and access controls. Namespaces can be used to segregate different parts of a network, allowing administrators to define policies and controls that apply only to specific sections of the network.

Nested Virtualization

Nested virtualization is a technique used to run virtual machines (VMs) within other VMs. This technology is useful for testing and development environments, as it allows VMs to be created and configured quickly and easily. Nested virtualization can also be used to isolate applications and services, preventing them from affecting other parts of the system.

Network Security

Refers to the protection of computer networks from unauthorized access or attacks. It involves implementing measures, such as firewalls, to prevent unauthorized access and intrusion detection systems to monitor network traffic and identify malicious activity. Other measures include implementing strong passwords, encryption, and virtual private networks (VPNs) to secure remote access to the network. Network security is essential to protect confidential information and prevent data breaches, which can be costly and damaging to organizations.

NIDS

Network Intrusion Detection System (NIDS) is a security technology that monitors network traffic for signs of malicious activity. NIDS solutions can analyze network packets and detect anomalies such as suspicious network traffic, malware infections, or attempts to exploit vulnerabilities in software. NIDS can also produce alerts or take action to stop an attack in progress.

NIST

The National Institute of Standards and Technology (NIST) is a government agency that develops and promotes technical standards, guidelines, and best practices for cybersecurity. NIST's Cybersecurity Framework is widely adopted by organizations to manage and reduce cybersecurity risks. The framework provides a set of guidelines and practices that enable organizations to improve their cybersecurity posture by identifying, assessing, and managing cybersecurity risks.

Non-repudiation

Non-repudiation is the ability to prove that a message or transaction was sent or received by a specific party and cannot be denied later. It is achieved through the use of digital signatures, which provide a means of validating the authenticity and integrity of electronic data. Non-repudiation is essential in legal and financial transactions, as it ensures that parties cannot dispute the validity of a transaction or deny their involvement.

NTP

Network Time Protocol (NTP) is a protocol used to synchronize clocks on computer systems and devices over a network. Accurate timekeeping is essential for security, as many security mechanisms, such as digital certificates and encryption, rely on accurate timestamps. NTP servers provide a reliable and accurate source of time for devices on a network.

OAuth

An open standard protocol for authorization used to provide third-party access to a user's account on a web application or service without sharing the user's login information. OAuth enables a user to grant temporary access permissions to another application or website without providing the login credentials. However, it can also be vulnerable to phishing attacks, where malicious actors trick users into granting access to their accounts.

Obfuscation

A technique used to obscure code or data to make it difficult for humans to read or understand. Obfuscation can make it more challenging for attackers to reverse engineer or exploit security vulnerabilities in software. However, it can also make it difficult for legitimate users to troubleshoot issues or modify the code.

One-Time Password

A temporary password that is valid for only one login session or transaction. One-time passwords can provide an additional layer of security for user authentication by mitigating the risk of password reuse, theft, or interception. They can be generated through physical or software-based token, such as a smartphone or hardware key.

Onion Router

A network protocol that enables anonymous communication on the internet by routing traffic through a series of servers to conceal the identity and location of the user. Onion routing is often used to access the dark web, where illegal activities can take place. While onion routing provides additional layers of anonymity, it can also hide the actions of cyber criminals and make it difficult for law enforcement to investigate cybercrimes.

Onion Services

A feature of the Tor privacy network that allows servers to be hosted on the internet while maintaining anonymity. Onion services have a randomized .onion domain name and can only be accessed using the Tor browser. While onion services can provide secrecy for legitimate purposes, such as whistleblowing or access to censorship-resistant information, they can also be used for malicious activities.

Open Source Software

A type of software whose source code is made available to the public for use, modification, and distribution. Open source software allows anyone to view and alter its source code, providing potential improvements and fixes to security vulnerabilities. Many cybersecurity tools and solutions are open source, benefiting from the contributions and scrutiny of a wider development community. However, it also means that malicious actors can potentially access and exploit code vulnerabilities.

Operating System

The software that manages computer hardware resources and provides services for computer programs. The security of an operating system is critical to cybersecurity, as vulnerabilities in the software can allow attackers to gain unauthorized access to systems or data.

Operations Security

A process used to identify and protect critical information that could be used against an organization's operations or personnel by hostile actors. Operations security involves identifying critical information, assessing the risks and vulnerabilities, and implementing safeguards to prevent exploitation or compromise. This can include measures such as reducing the amount of exposed data, limiting access to sensitive information, and training staff to detect and avoid security threats.

Out-of-Band Management

A type of remote management for networking devices that uses a separate communication channel from the regular data channel. Out-of-band management allows administrators to access and manage devices when the regular data channel is down or compromised. This can provide an additional layer of security and reliability to network infrastructure.

Over-the-air Updates

A method of updating software or firmware on devices wirelessly, without the need for physical access. Over-the-air updates can provide a quick and convenient way to distribute security patches or software upgrades, reducing the risk of vulnerabilities being exploited. However, they can also be subject to interception or tampering if the update process is not properly secured.

Password hygiene

The practice of creating strong, unique and complex passwords and changing them regularly to reduce the risk of unauthorized access. Password hygiene involves avoiding common passwords, using a password manager to store and generate passwords, and enabling two-factor authentication to add an additional layer of protection to online accounts. Poor password hygiene is one of the leading causes of cyber attacks such as credential stuffing or brute force attacks.

Patch

A security patch is a software update designed to address vulnerabilities or bugs in the system. Patches are essential to maintain the security of software applications, networks, or devices by fixing flaws that could be exploited by hackers to gain unauthorized access or control. It is critical to apply patches promptly as many cyber attacks exploit known vulnerabilities that have not been patched.

Patch Management

The practice of regularly identifying, testing, and deploying security patches to address known vulnerabilities and protect systems from cyber attacks. Patch management involves monitoring for new vulnerabilities, testing patches for compatibility, prioritizing critical patches, and deploying them without causing disruptions to the system. A robust patch management process is critical to mitigate the risk of cyber attacks that exploit unpatched vulnerabilities.

Penetration testing

A type of ethical hacking where cybersecurity experts simulate an attack on a system, network or application to identify vulnerabilities and weaknesses. Penetration testing helps organizations to assess their security posture and identify potential entry points for cybercriminals. It provides insights into the effectiveness of existing security controls and helps organizations to improve their security defenses.

Perimeter security

The practice of securing the network perimeter to prevent unauthorized access or attacks from cybercriminals. Perimeter security typically involves firewalls, intrusion detection and prevention systems, and network access controls. The goal of perimeter security is to create a secure boundary between trusted and untrusted networks, to filter traffic based on policies, and block any malicious traffic that could harm network resources or data. Perimeter security is essential but not sufficient to protect against advanced threats like zero-day exploits or targeted attacks.

Phishing

A type of cyber attack where hackers impersonate a trustworthy entity like a bank, government agency or company, and attempt to deceive unsuspecting victims into providing sensitive information such as usernames, passwords or credit card details. Phishing attacks typically occur through emails or text messages with links to fake login pages, or attachments that contain malicious software.

Privacy

The protection of personal information from unauthorized access, use, or disclosure. With the increasing amount of data being shared online, cybersecurity experts recommend individuals to take steps to protect their privacy, such as using strong passwords, enabling two-factor authentication, and avoiding oversharing personal information on social media. Companies must also comply with privacy regulations like GDPR, HIPAA or CCPA to protect their customers' data.

Protocol

A set of rules or guidelines that define how data is transmitted, received, and processed between devices, software applications, or systems. In cybersecurity, protocols are used to ensure secure communication and data exchange, such as SSL/TLS for secure web browsing, HTTPS for secure data transmission, SMTP for email, or SSH for remote access. Protocols need to be secure, reliable, and interoperable, and must be updated regularly to address new threats and vulnerabilities. Malicious actors can exploit vulnerabilities in protocols, especially those that are not widely adopted or poorly implemented, to gain unauthorized access or bypass security controls.

Proxy

A intermediary server that acts as an intermediary between a device and the internet. Proxies can be used to hide the IP address and location of the device, making it more difficult for hackers to identify or target the device. Proxies can also be used to access blocked or restricted websites, bypass content filters, or improve internet speed by caching frequently accessed web pages. However, proxies can also be used to conduct malicious activities like accessing illegal content or distributing malware.

Public-Key Cryptography

A data encryption method that uses two keys

QoS (Quality of Service)

A measure of the performance of a computer network or internet connection in relation to specific requirements. In cybersecurity, QoS is used to ensure that the network has the necessary bandwidth and resources to support security protocols and maintain data integrity.

Quantum Computing

The emerging technology that uses quantum mechanics to create powerful computers that can break down complex algorithms and codes associated with cybersecurity. Quantum computers use quantum bits or qubits, which offer a more powerful computing system than traditional binary bits.

Quantum Key Distribution (QKP)

A high-security encryption method that uses the principles of quantum physics to share encryption keys securely. In cybersecurity, QKP is used to ensure the secure transmission of sensitive data, such as financial or confidential information, between two or more parties.

Quarantine

The process of isolating a potentially infected or compromised device or file to prevent the spread of malware or other security threats. In cybersecurity, quarantining may be used to prevent the spread of viruses, trojans, and other malware by isolating infected devices or files until they can be safely removed or deleted.

Qubes OS

A security-focused operating system that uses virtualization to isolate various applications and programs to prevent security breaches. In cybersecurity, Qubes OS can be used to create secure and isolated environments for running sensitive applications, such as online banking or healthcare record management.

Query

A process of searching for information or data from a database or computer system. In cybersecurity, queries are often used to identify and isolate potential security threats, identify stolen data, and prevent further data breaches.

Query Optimization

The process of optimizing queries to improve the performance of a database or computer system. In cybersecurity, query optimization can be used to identify potential vulnerabilities, improve the efficiency of security protocols, and ensure the integrity of stored data.

Quick Response (QR) Code

A two-dimensional barcode that is commonly used for product promotions, advertising, and marketing. In cybersecurity, QR codes can be used to store and share sensitive information, such as payment details or login credentials, which can be easily stolen by cybercriminals.

Quiet Period

A period of time during which a company's insiders are prohibited from trading the company's securities. In cybersecurity, quiet periods may be implemented to prevent insider trading based on confidential information related to cybersecurity incidents or data breaches.

Quine-McCluskey Algorithm

A Boolean algebra optimization algorithm used for digital circuits and computer applications. In cybersecurity, the Quine-McCluskey algorithm can be used to simplify complex security protocols, automate security tasks, and improve overall system efficiency.

Ransomware

Type of malicious software that encrypts data and files, preventing the user from accessing them. The attacker demands payment, usually in cryptocurrency, to restore access. Ransomware attacks are becoming more common and can have devastating consequences for individuals and organizations, including loss of data and financial loss.

Recovery Time Objective (RTO)

The amount of time it takes to restore a system or service after failure. The RTO is an important metric for assessing business continuity and disaster recovery plans. The shorter the RTO, the faster a system or service can be restored, minimizing downtime and reducing the impact of a disaster.

Redundancy

The practice of using multiple systems, devices, or components to ensure that in the event of a failure, the system can continue to function. Redundancy is critical for maintaining system availability and minimizing downtime. Redundancy can also increase security by providing backups in case of a security breach.

Remote Access

The ability to access a computer or network from a remote location. Remote access can be facilitated through VPNs, Remote Desktop Protocol (RDP), and other tools. Remote access is convenient, but it can also create security risks if proper security measures are not in place.

Remote Wiping

A security feature that allows a user to erase data from a lost or stolen device remotely. Remote wiping can be used to prevent sensitive data from falling into the wrong hands and can be useful in the event of a security breach. However, remote wiping should be used with caution to avoid accidental data loss or damage to the device.

Reputation Management

The practice of monitoring and managing an individual or organization's online reputation. Reputation management includes monitoring social media, blogs, and other websites for negative comments, reviews, or articles. Maintaining a positive online reputation is important for individuals and organizations to build trust and credibility.

Risk Assessment

Process of identifying, analyzing, and evaluating risks to an organization's information security. A risk assessment helps to identify vulnerabilities and threats and develop strategies for mitigating or managing them. It includes reviewing security policies, procedures, and practices to identify areas of weakness or potential vulnerabilities.

Rogue Access Point

An unauthorized wireless access point that is connected to a wired network without authorization. Rogue access points can provide a point of entry for attackers to access the network and steal sensitive information. Organizations should monitor their wireless networks for rogue access points and take steps to remove them.

Rootkit

A type of malware that allows hackers to gain unauthorized access to a system and remain undetected. A rootkit modifies the operating system to hide its presence and can perform a variety of malicious activities, including stealing data, controlling the system, and installing other malware.

Router

A device that connects multiple networks and directs data traffic between them. Routers are used to manage network traffic and ensure that data is delivered to its intended recipient. Routers can also provide security by acting as a firewall and blocking unauthorized access to a network.

Security Breach

An incident where an unauthorized individual gains access to a system or data. A security breach can be intentional or unintentional, and it can result in data theft, destruction, or unauthorized access to sensitive information.

Social Engineering

A method of manipulating individuals to access confidential information by posing as a trustworthy source. Social engineering tactics can include phishing, baiting, and pretexting.

Spam

Unsolicited messages sent through email or messaging platforms. Spam can contain malware, phishing attempts, or unwanted advertising messages.

Spear Phishing

A targeted phishing attack that is personalized to an individual or organization. Spear phishing attempts to extract sensitive information through the use of social engineering tactics, such as posing as a trusted contact or authority figure.

Spyware

A type of malware that is designed to collect information about a computer user without their knowledge. Spyware can record keystrokes, track internet usage, and monitor user activity.

SQL Injection

A hacking technique used to gain access to a database server. SQL Injection involves inserting malicious code or commands into a database query to extract, modify or delete data.

SSL

Secure Socket Layer is a technology that encrypts data sent over the internet to prevent unauthorized access or interception. SSL is used for secure online transactions and data transfers.

Tcp/Ip

The set of communication protocols used for transmitting data over the internet. TCP (Transmission Control Protocol) is responsible for breaking data down into packets and ensuring its reliable delivery, while IP (Internet Protocol) is responsible for routing packets to their intended destination.

Test Environment

A separate, isolated environment used for testing software, applications, or other system components before they are deployed in a production environment. A well-designed test environment can help identify and fix vulnerabilities and ensure that systems and applications are secure and functional before they are released to users.

Threat Hunting

A proactive approach to cybersecurity that involves actively searching for hidden or emerging threats that may have evaded traditional security measures. Threat hunting often involves analyzing logs and network activity in order to identify abnormal behavior indicating a potential breach or attack.

Threat Intelligence

The information and insights gathered about potential threats to an organization's security, including details about attacker tactics, malware signatures, and exploits. Threat intelligence is used to identify potential risks and vulnerabilities, and to develop targeted, proactive responses to cyber threats.

Threat Vector

The method by which a cyber attack enters your system or network. Vulnerabilities such as outdated software, weak passwords, or infected devices can all provide entry points for hackers. A thorough understanding of threat vectors is crucial in developing effective cybersecurity strategies.

Tokenization

The process of replacing sensitive data like credit card numbers or passwords with non-sensitive equivalents, known as tokens, that are unique to each user or transaction. Tokenization helps protect against data breaches by reducing the amount of valuable information stored on a network.

Traceroute

A command-line tool used to trace the path of data from one network device to another. Traceroute can help diagnose connectivity issues and identify the specific network devices or routers that may be causing problems.

Trojan

A type of malware that disguises itself as legitimate software in order to trick users into downloading or installing it, allowing attackers to gain control of the victim's device or network. Trojans can be very difficult to detect as they are often designed to operate silently in the background.

Trust Model

A framework that establishes trust between different entities within a system or network. It defines the roles, permissions, and trust relationships among users, systems, and applications. A well-designed trust model can help prevent unauthorized access and protect sensitive data.

Two-Factor Authentication

A security process that requires users to provide two forms of identification in order to access an account, system, or network. It adds an extra layer of protection beyond a simple password, as it typically involves a physical item (like a phone or token) combined with a regular password.

Virtualization

A technology that enables the creation of virtual computers, software, or networks, run on a single physical machine. Virtualization can enhance cybersecurity by running multiple operating systems, applications or software on a single machine, separating them from the host operating system, and minimizing risks of data breach or system crashes.

Virus

A type of malicious software or malware that infects a computer or network by replicating itself and spreading to other computers or files. Viruses can cause data corruption, system crashes, or theft of sensitive information. Preventive measures such as regularly updating antivirus software, avoiding suspicious email attachments, and not downloading files or software from untrusted sources can minimize the risk of virus infection.

Virus Signature

A unique electronic fingerprint or pattern of malicious code that antivirus software uses to identify a particular virus. When a virus signature is recognized by antivirus software, it can stop or quarantine the file immediately, preventing further infection or spread of the virus. Antivirus software must be regularly updated to recognize new virus signatures to be effective.

Voice phishing or "Vishing"

A type of social engineering attack in which cyber attackers use voice or phone calls to solicit sensitive information from victims. These attacks are often disguised as legitimate institutions such as banks or credit card companies, and exploit human trust to gather confidential information. To avoid being a victim of vishing, it is important to verify the legitimacy of the caller, never provide personal information over the phone unless certain it is secure and legitimate, and report suspicious calls.

Volume Shadow Copy Service

A Windows operating system tool that creates backup images of system data, files, and applications. This tool allows users to restore lost files or data in the event of a cyberattack, ransomware attack or other data loss. It is recommended that users keep a backup copy of their data on an external hard drive or cloud storage.

VPN (Virtual Private Network)

A secure and encrypted network connection that allows users to access the internet or a private network remotely. VPNs provide privacy and anonymity by hiding their IP address, location, and online activity from cyber attackers and other third parties. They are commonly used by remote workers, travelers, and individuals seeking to bypass geo-restricted content. However, users must choose a reputable VPN provider as some free or low-cost VPNs may log and sell user data, defeating the purpose of using a VPN.

VPN Kill Switch

A security feature provided by some VPN providers that automatically terminates an internet connection if the VPN connection is lost, preventing any data transmission outside the secure VPN tunnel. This feature helps to protect users' privacy and security by preventing exposure of their IP address and online activity to cyber attackers even if the VPN connection is interrupted.

VPN Tunnelling

A secure and encrypted connection established between a user's device and a VPN server, creating a virtual tunnel for data to travel through. All data transmitted between the user and the VPN server is encrypted and protected from being accessed by cyber attackers or third parties. Users can choose from a variety of VPN protocols to use, including OpenVPN, IPSec, and L2TP.

Vulnerability

A weakness or flaw in a system, software, or network that can be exploited by cyber attackers to gain unauthorized access or steal confidential information. These can be caused by outdated software, unsecured databases, or even human error. Cybersecurity professionals constantly monitor and patch vulnerabilities to prevent cyberattacks and data breaches. Regular software updates, strong passwords, and proper configuration of firewalls and other security measures can also help to mitigate vulnerability risks.

Vulnerability Assessment

The process of evaluating and identifying vulnerabilities in a computer or network infrastructure. This involves scanning devices, software, and network configurations to identify vulnerabilities that can be exploited by cyber attackers. The results of vulnerability assessments are used to prioritize and implement security measures such as software patches, configuration changes, or additional security controls.

War Dialing

War dialing is a technique used to find unprotected dial-up modems. Attackers will use automated software to dial a range of phone numbers in order to find modems that are connected to computers. Once a vulnerable modem is found, the attacker can gain access to the connected computer and potentially steal sensitive data.

Watering Hole Attack

A watering hole attack is a type of cyberattack that targets a specific group of individuals by infecting a website that they regularly visit. The attacker is able to infect the site with malware and when the target visits the site, their computer is infected with the malicious software.

Web Application Firewall

A web application firewall (WAF) is a security tool that monitors and filters HTTP traffic to a web application. A WAF can block attacks such as SQL injection, cross-site scripting, and session hijacking. A WAF can be configured to block incoming traffic that does not match a set of rules or patterns.

Web of Trust

Web of trust is a popular browser extension that allows users to rate and review websites based on their trustworthiness. The extension uses a crowdsourced rating system to provide users with information about the safety of websites they visit. The tool helps users avoid malicious websites and protect their privacy while browsing the web.

Whaling

Whaling is a type of phishing attack that targets high-profile individuals such as executives or senior management. The attackers often impersonate a trusted source such as a colleague or supplier and use social engineering tactics to trick the victim into divulging sensitive information or money.

White Hat Hacker

A white hat hacker is a cybersecurity professional who uses their skills to identify vulnerabilities in systems in order to improve their security. White hat hackers are ethically and legally obliged to use their skills for good purposes and obtain permission before conducting any security testing.

Wifi Sniffing

Wi-Fi sniffing is a type of cyberattack where attackers intercept and monitor wireless traffic. Attackers can use various tools to listen in on wireless traffic to find sensitive information such as login credentials or credit card numbers. Wi-Fi sniffing can be mitigated by using encrypted connections and avoiding unsecured public Wi-Fi networks.

Wireless Intrusion Prevention System

A wireless intrusion prevention system (WIPS) is a security tool that monitors wireless networks for potential security breaches. WIPS can detect rogue access points, unauthorized devices, and other anomalies in the wireless network. WIPS can also automatically block traffic from unauthorized devices.

WORM

A worm is a type of malware that replicates itself in order to spread throughout a network or device. Worms do not need to rely on a user to spread and can cause harm by overloading networks or stealing sensitive data. Worms are often spread through email attachments or security vulnerabilities in software.

WPA2

Wi-Fi Protected Access 2 is a security protocol used to secure wireless networks. WPA2 uses encryption to ensure that only authorized users can access the network and protects against unauthorized access and eavesdropping.